Super Calm Sleepers

Super Calm Sleepers

Table Of Contents

Foreword

Sleep is defined as a state when the motor activity and senses are suspended; there is partial or total unconsciousness, and the voluntary muscles of the body are not active. It is more reversible than coma or hibernation, yet responds less to any kind of stimulus than silent wakefulness. Sleep is very important, as it is the rest cycle of the body. Get all the info you need here.

Super Serenity Sleepers
The Guide To Sleeping Productively

Chapter 1:

Introduction

Synopsis

Doctors say that this cycle is a heightened anabolic state—a certain period when the body produces new nervous and muscular tissue and bone. To put it simply, this is a period when the body grows and being repaired.

The Basics

Sleep is triggered by a group of hormones in the body. These hormones react to cues within the body and in the environment. There is an approximate 80 percent of sleep time without dreams. This stage of dreamless sleep is referred to as NREM which stands for non-rapid eye movement. Dreams occur primarily during rapid eye movement or REM.

During non-rapid eye movement sleep or NREM, the breathing and heart rates are slow and the blood pressure goes down. Based on the Rechtschaffen and Kales standardization of the year 1968, NREM was divided into 4 stages. However, it has been reduced to 3 by The American Academy of Sleep Machine in 2007.

Stage 1 – This stage mostly occurs in the start of sleep wherein theta wave emerges while alpha waves vanish. Those who are aroused from this stage believe that they have been completely awake. It is also in this stage when the body experiences hypnic jerks.

Stage 2 – In this stage, dreaming is rare and no eye movement takes place. The sleeper may also be wakened easily.

Stage 3 – This is also referred to as slow-wave sleep of SWS, wherein deep sleep takes place. This is also the stage when dreaming occurs. However, the content of slow-wave sleep is likely to be less memorable, less vivid and disconnected than those in rapid eye movement sleep.

On the other hand, rapid eye movement sleep also known as REM, is a normal phase of sleep making up between20% and 25% of the whole sleep time. Apart from the swift movement of the eyes, this stage is also characterized by low muscle tone.

Human beings usually experience 4 to 5 REM sleep periods during a usual full session of sleep, and the last is longer than the first one. According to sleep experts, the brain neurons are as dynamic during rapid eye movement sleep as they are when the body is awake. However, atonia, a relaxed state of the skeletal muscles, makes the body paralyzed during REM.

In the succeeding chapters, you will know more about sleep and how to make the most out of it.

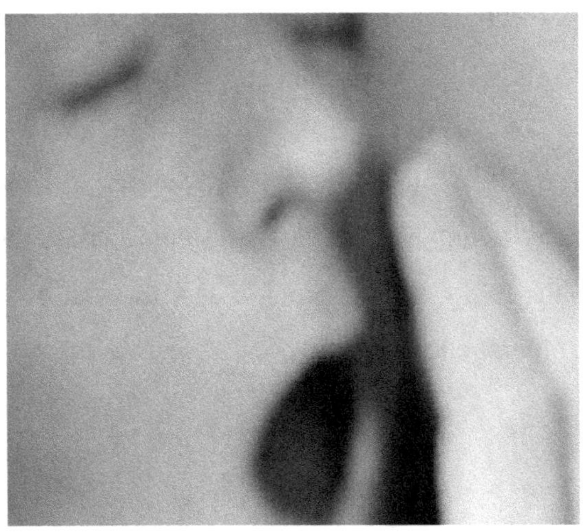

Chapter 2:

The Importance of the Right Sleep

Synopsis

According to National Sleep Foundation, all people need to get the right sleep because this is how the body recuperates all the energy it has lost after a tiring day.

Well, this is a no-brainer, so you don't need an expert organization to tell you how important sleep is. Some of the common signs of lack of sleep are incapability to multitask, disinhibition, slowed speech, impaired memory, moodiness and irritability.

Disinhibition pertains to poor risk evaluation and lack of self-control. It commonly results to a reduced ability in managing or editing their response to a certain situation.

The amount of sleep humans need greatly varies with every person, yet on average, an adult must have 8 sleeping hours. Some people have the ability to do well in school or at work with only 6 hours of sleep, while others require 10.

How Sleep Deprivation Can Affect the Body

Psychologists and scientists who conducted study on sleep disorders have found out that sleep deprivation can have an adverse effect on the following:

Metabolic Functions – The processes required for a living organism's maintenance.

The Immune System – This system is a defense mechanism that is made up of a large network of organs, tissues, and cells working together to give the body shield from any infectious organisms like toxins, parasites, viruses, microbes and bacteria.

Cardiovascular System – This system comprises of capillaries, blood and heart vessels, veins and arteries. It transports gases, metabolic wastes, hormones and foods to and from the cells.

Nervous System – The brain, an integral part of the nervous system, controls everything concerning the body such as fundamental functions, sensations, emotions, thoughts and actions.

There are so many reasons as to why people need to get a good night's sleep. In fact, it is not just designed for the physical health, but for the mental, social, emotional and spiritual health as well.
By simply having a good quality sleep every night, the quality of your life will also improve. However, this will only be possible if you will fix

your lifestyle and eat a balanced diet. In other words, the quality of sleep you will get will depend on the everyday choices you make and on how you live your life.

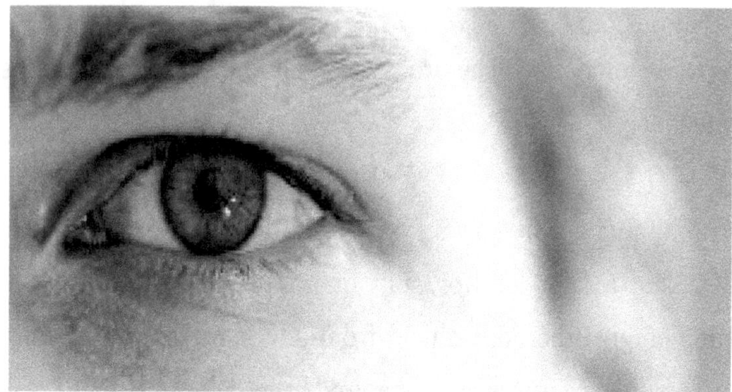

Chapter 3:

Watch What You Drink

Synopsis

Have you ever noticed that you feel energized or sleepy after drinking certain things? Well, that is simply because the drinks you consume can affect the quality of your sleep. Just like other human beings, you have the right to sleep soundly at night. So, read the succeeding paragraphs to know the worst drinks that will rob you off a good night's sleep.

Drinks

Coffee

You surely know for a fact that the main ingredient in coffee is caffeine. This is popularly known as the most common drug in the world because it is a stimulant which works by increasing the body's energy levels. Research shows that coffee drinkers suffer from a wide range of sleep disorders such as apnea, insomnia and narcolepsy.

If you can't resist drinking coffee, maybe now is the right time for you to give it up. Yes, it can make you energetic the whole day, but it can make you feel restless the moment you go to bed. If you don't want to be a living zombie, say goodbye to coffee now!

Alcohol

It is believed that drinking alcohol before going to bed will make you feel relaxed and easier to enter dreamland. This may be true to others, but studies show that this beverage can disrupt sleep and increase your tendency to snore. According to London Sleep Centre scientists, it acts as a sedative, but can disrupt the body's sleeping pattern.

Those who sleep under the influence will feel like they have been in a deep sleep, buy they have actually been deprived of rapid eye movement (REM) sleep.

What is alarming nowadays is that so many people have become dependent on alcohol in order to sleep. Experts claim that this is very dangerous to the body because it can lead to addiction and worse, insomnia.

The Relationship of Alcohol and Snoring

Many people think that by drinking too much alcohol, they will immediately fall into a deep sleep. As aforementioned, since it is a sedative, it can cheat the body out of good quality sleep. This is the reason why people who drink alcohol still get tired right after 8 to 9 hours of sleep.

Studies show that alcohol can turn a non-habitual snorer to a habitual one and worse, it can increase his/her tendency to suffer from apnea. This is because alcohol makes the tissue around the nasal passages and throat relaxed, thus making the soft tissue to vibrate and move.

So, what does this study mean? Well, if you have an important meeting or event to attend to the next morning, the best decision you could ever make is to forget about the nightcap. If you want your life to be on the right track, you should say no to the things that can harm your body. Alcohol is one of them.

Chapter 4:

Understand That Exercise Is Important For Sleep

Synopsis

One of the most common sleep disorders that are experienced by millions of people around the world is insomnia. This is defined as the incapability to sleep, not depending upon the number of your sleeping hours, but on your sleep's quality and how you feel the moment you wake up in the morning.

Thus, even if you were able to sleep 8 hours during the night, but feel tired when you wake up, that means you have insomnia.

People suffering from this pesky sleeping disorder usually resort to medication, as it is convenient and offers quick results. However, the major drawback of medicines is that they can be very addictive.

Good thing, there are some healthy alternatives that can help you to be free from insomnia without spending a fortune and exposing your body to risks and side effects.

Thanks to Exercises

By simply stretching your muscles and moving your joints, you will no longer feel like you are a living zombie due to the inability to sleep. The following are some of the most ideal exercises that will give your body a boost and set your sleeping pattern on the right track:

Stress Relaxation Exercises - The key to having a good night's sleep is relaxation. One of the most common and effective relaxation strategies is to count backwards. In doing so, the excessively active neuron activity in the brain will be deactivated, so you will become bored and go off to a deep slumber. But wait. If you don't want to count backwards, just count sheep instead.

Breathing Exercise – You can also perform a deep breathing exercise involving the ribcage, lower back, lower abdomen and chest. By simply inhaling deeply and fully, the parasympathetic nervous system which controls relaxation will be affected. This will result in sleep and comfort. In addition, since you are inhaling more oxygen amount, the supply of your blood increases within your brain and body. As a result, the essential nutrients which aid you to sleep better, properly flows to your brain. This exercise is taught in Art of Living and Reiki.

Muscle Relaxation Exercise – This is by far the simplest exercise that can help you avoid insomnia. All you need to do is tense your muscles to the toes and relax them suddenly. When all your muscle groups are relaxed, you will not find it hard to enter dreamland. Acute stress will cause your muscles to have high tension. So, when your muscles are relaxed and tensed, the level of tension will drop below the normal level, thus helping you achieve a higher level of relaxation. However, you must be comfortable prior to performing this kind of exercise.

Meditation – This is another effective exercise that can treat your insomnia. All you have to do is work on the basic meditation aspect whereby you are concentrating on your breathing, on an object or on a word. This activity will pave the way for you to have peace of mind and relaxation. Bear in mind that visual imagery is a great strategy that will aid you to distract your mind from your current problems.

If you are an insomniac, the abovementioned exercises will pave the way for you to experience the deepest and most relaxing slumber ever. So, why don't you exercise your mind and your body regularly? You will surely love the benefits.

Chapter 5:

Watch What You Eat

Synopsis

Sleeping and eating have more in common than their shared standing as fundamental biological functions. The quality of your sleep has a great impact to your eating pattern; eating certain foods can have a great impact to the quality and time of your sleep patterns. See the relationship? Therefore, eating a balanced and healthy diet can enhance your sleep, and vice versa.

In the succeeding paragraphs, you will be able to know the best and worst foods that can positively or negatively affect your sleep time and quality.

The Foods

Proteins and Carbohydrates

Foods rich in carbohydrates like breads and pastas can make you fall asleep easily. They perfectly work with proteins to stimulate sleepiness, making combinations like cracker and cheese, cereal with milk, or toasted peanut butter great bedtime snacks. However, eating a large meal with a high amount of carbohydrates before bedtime can make you feel tired. You should also limit your protein consumption before going to bed because foods rich in it contain tyrosine, a type of amino acid that rouse the activity of the brain.

Dairy Foods

Yogurt, cheese and milk are some of the foods that are rich in tryptophan, a type of amino acid that converts to serotonin and melatonin—both considered as good sleep inducers.

Peanuts, Poultry, Bananas and Oats

Just like dairy foods, peanuts, poultry, bananas and oats also contain tryptophan. Low-protein and high-carbohydrate meals are also believed to increase tryptophan levels.

Spicy Foods

These foods usually stimulate heart burn, which may keep you awake all night long. So, if your body is not quite comfortable with spicy foods, then you need to avoid them because your sleep quality will be at stake.

Caffeine and Energy Dips

The energy of the body naturally flows and ebbs throughout the day. In accordance with the National Sleep Foundation, there are common times for sleepiness—specifically 2 a.m. and 2 p.m. Taking a nap, especially in the afternoon, will help balance your energy and guarantee a normal duration of sleep at night. It is also crucial to plan caffeine intake around your sleep patterns. Just like sugar, a high amount of caffeine makes valleys and peaks of energy that may disrupt your sleep patterns. Drinking a small amount of caffeine throughout the day is also proven helpful when it comes to sustaining energy.

Circadian Rhythm

Primeval survival intuitions associated with food availability can reorganize the patterns of your sleep or circadian rhythm. By simply fasting for about 16 hours will trigger the brain that food is in short supply. Upon eating the food at a certain time that you wish to be awake, the body will think that food is really present during that time, and will reorganize the pattern of your sleep. This is by far one of the most functional tricks that will help alter a sleep schedule for a time zone change, exercise routine or job change.

Now that you already know that what you eat can positively or negatively affect your sleep pattern, you should begin watching your diet.

Chapter 6:

Learn the Importance of Winding Down

Synopsis

One of the things that people can never escape in this world is stress. In order for your body to be recharged for the next day's challenges, you have to de-stress and get a good night's sleep.

In accordance with Mark Stibich, Ph.D, sleeping is an important function in keeping the body strong and up for anything. To be specific, it is responsible for cellular repair, muscular repair, energy, memory, concentration, etc.

Constant sleep deprivation increases the body's risk for having infections, cardiovascular disease, diabetes, obesity and other diseases. With the different distractions in life, having good quality sleep every night can be a difficult one for some people. Therefore, it is important to wind down.

The following are some of the best ways to wind down:

Turn Off What Must Be Turned Off – 2 hours before bedtime, you have to turn off your computer and TV. Did you know that the stimulation coming from this kind of electromagnetic stress will keep your mind ticking into the late hours of the night, causing you to be more aggravated and stressed? Don't abuse yourself, so just put off for tomorrow your online activities.

Pamper Yourself – After a hard day's work, you need to pamper yourself by simply taking hot bath or shower. The warm water can relieve your achy and tired muscles. In order to soothe your entire body completely, you can also add in lavender shower gel into the tub. To make your bathing moment more special and invigorating, set the bathroom with scented candles. When you are done, apply your favorite lotion to your skin and go to bed. But don't forget to dry your hair.

Breathe Deeply – Before going to bed, you need to engage in meditation or a deep breathing exercise. Doing so will aid in lowering your heart rate, thus resulting in a more relaxed and calm state of mind. In every deep and long breath you take, you can also have a chance to release all your physical and mental stress.

Take Time to Read – Before going to bed, try to read your favorite magazine or book. This will not just take your mind to a positive state, but will make you sleepy as well. Therefore, you will fall into deep slumber more easily.

Drink Tea – A hot tea prior to bed will surely soothe you and invigorate your senses. Its warmth will help slow the body's system and lull you into deep sleep. Don't ever dare to drink coffee because it will make you awake all night due to its high caffeine content.

One of the best ways to give yourself a treat is through winding down. By following the ideas mentioned in this article, you will surely have the most relaxing and deepest slumber ever. Why don't you start this evening?

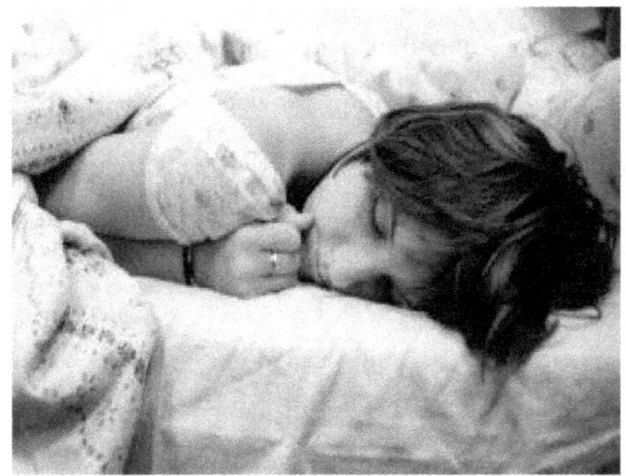

Chapter 7:

Synopsis

One of the most essential rhythms in the human body is the sleep schedule. Every 24 hours, the human body needs 6-8 hours of sleep to refresh and repair itself for the next 24 hours. Unluckily, there are things, events and circumstances interfering with the body's sleep patterns and it may be required for people to alter their sleeping habits permanently or temporarily. By simply understanding your sleeping habits and practicing self-discipline, you will learn the art of setting a sleep schedule.

The following are the ways to do that:

Eating Light Dinner or Nothing at All – One of the most ideal ways to set your sleep schedule is through fasting for 16 hours until the next morning when you consume a protein-rich meal. Studies show that fasting can effectively reset the body clock.

Avoid Stimulants – Depending on your body's size, the amount of food you consume and your health, caffeine, one of the most popular stimulants can stay active in your body for up to 5-10 hours right after the preliminary consumption. Likewise, nicotine must not also be introduced to the body right after dinner.

Say No to Alcohol – By nature, alcohol is a sedative. This means that it has the ability to slow down your body. Yes, this may aid you to fall asleep faster, but it can also slow down your metabolic process and disrupt with your mind during its sleep phase.

Wait Until Bedtime to Turn In – One of the best ways to refresh your batteries when you have a steady sleep schedule is taking naps. However, they are proven counter-productive when attempting to alter your sleeping patterns. Do not take a nap during daytime, so that you can fall asleep easier at the right time later.

Identify Your Preferred Waking Time – If you are altering your sleep schedule, so that you can wake up early in the morning for work or for school, you most likely want to wake up an hour prior to departure.

Calculate Sleeping Time – Most people want 6-8 hours of sleep every night. However, the exact period of sleep varies from person to person. In order for you to wake up at your preferred waking time, you have to sleep at the right time. For instance, if you only need to sleep for 6 hours and you desire to wake up at 5a.m, then you have to sleep at exactly 11p.m.

Minimize or Eliminate Distractions – You need to turn off the lights in your room before you go to bed because they will certainly distract you. You can also utilize earplugs if you can't sleep because of your noisy neighbor or the pesky sound created by the crickets. Setting up your sleep schedule involves sleeping at the right time without any distraction.

Change Your Sleep Schedule Slowly – If you usually wake up at 10:00 a.m. in the morning but want to wake up at 5:00 a.m., making the alteration overnight will be counterproductive.

If you want to be more productive at work or to have a better quality of life, setting up a sleep schedule is the key.

Chapter 8:

Understand How to Make Your Room Sleep Friendly

Synopsis

There are several factors that can greatly affect your sleep cycle and quality; one of which is your room. This is the reason why you need to make it the most comfortable and beautiful place in the world. By making your room sleep-friendly, you will always have a deep slumber every night or each time you take a nap.

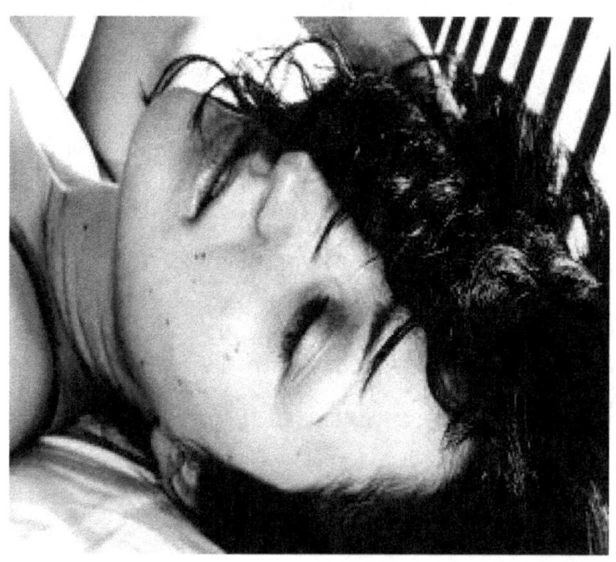

Changing the Environment for Better Sleep Quality

The sleep environment could be one of the impediments to good sleeping habits for several reasons. First, do you really like the place where you sleep? Can you consider your bedroom a relaxing and peaceful place? If your answer to these questions is no, then you should start remodeling or cleaning it up now. The following are the best ideas that can help you turn your room into a more sleep-friendly place:

Remove All the Clutter and Organize Your Stuff – The sad thing is that several people's bedrooms look dull and messy like a closet that is out of control. By removing all the clutter, it will be a better place. So, spend time picking up all your dirty clothes and putting away the clean piles of your laundry. If you work at home, you need to separate your sleep area from your workspace because this is a great distraction.

Evaluate the Mattress – The mattress is essential to good sleep, but it can also be costly and may not be included in your budget. Yet, if you are still sleeping on an old and damaged mattress, prioritize buying a new one. In shopping, make sure that you choose the right mattress carefully to get the best of both worlds. By simply choosing a luxurious bed linen set, you will always have a deep sleep.

Set the Right Room Temperature – Ensure that your room has the right temperature because if not, the quality of your sleep will be negatively affected. Most people want to have a cooler room because it helps them to fall into deep sleep faster.

Sound – Another thing you need to consider is the sound in your room. Do you fall asleep faster when you listen to mellow songs or do you want complete silence? Whatever you want, you need to give it to yourself. If you want to listen to a relaxing sound or white noise as what they call it, then investing in a sound machine would be a great decision. This machine offers the best nature sounds like the sound of the ocean, the rainfall and the rainforest. However, if you want silence, make sure that your sound-generating appliances are turned off and your windows are closed. You can also purchase earplugs.

Lighting - To make your room a more sleep-friendly place, you also need to check your lighting. If you can't sleep with the light on, then turn off everything. However, if you are not comfortable in total darkness, purchase a lampshade.

These are just some of the ways on how to make your room a sleep-friendly place. When everything is already in order, you can give yourself the best relaxation treat ever. So, why don't you transform your room into a lovely place now?

Chapter 9:

Learn How to Shut Your Brain Off

Synopsis

Do you feel like getting to bed is a nightmare? For most people, as soon as it is already time for bed, their mind starts buzzing. They experience crazy racing thoughts that soon lead to worry thoughts. As a result, they are not able to function the moment they wake up the next morning because they had a poor sleep. When this continues, it would become a vicious cycle.

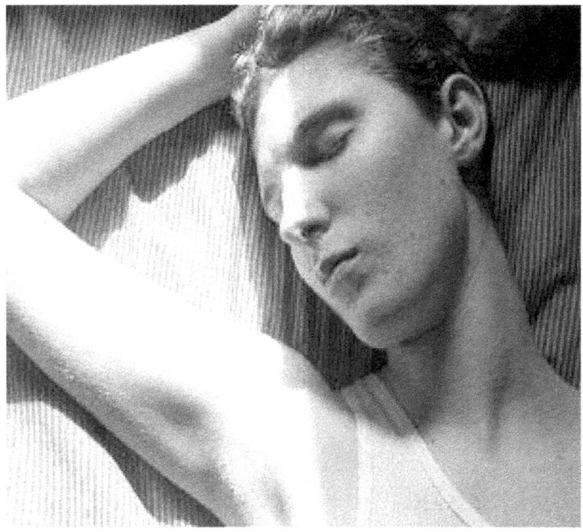

Making the Right Associations

According to Sleep Health Centers chief medical officer, Lawrence Epstein, M.D., it is possible to make the right associations to sleep well even though the brain does not have a button for deactivation. The following are the ways that can help you do it:

Know that Sleep is Important – Sleep is the best form of rest that you could ever give to yourself. However, if you are deprived of it, you will face various issues such as anxiety. It will also hinder you from functioning at your best whether at home, in school or at work. According to experts, lack of sleep can also pose several health problems such as diabetes, stroke and hypertension.

Regular Sleep Schedule – The key to have a good sleep quality is through going to bed and waking up early. Dr. Epstein also points out that the best promoter of being able to sleep well is being synchronized with the body's inner clock or circadian rhythm.

Winding Down prior to Bed – Along with regular wake/sleep schedule, one of the most ideal ways to get your sleep schedule back on track is through winding down prior to bed. You need to let go of all the negative thoughts you have in mind in order for you to enter dreamland quickly.

Make a Pre-sleep Routine – By simply creating an ideal pre-sleep routine, you will be able to establish association between your sleep and certain activities. By simply doing relaxing things such as taking a hot shower or reading books before bedtime, you can set your body in the mood to sleep. Apart from that, it will also give you the energy you need the moment you get up the next morning.

Write Down All Your Worries – If you are disturbed by racing thoughts before you go to bed, you need to write down all the things that make you worry during your free time. In doing so, you can at least let them go. However, don't do this just before you go to bed because it will heighten your worries.

Use Your Bed for Intimacy and Sleep – You also need to make a clear association between your sleep and bed according to Dr. Epstein. He also advises that when you have some troubles sleeping, you can read your favorite books or magazines but not in the bed. Similarly, he also discourages using the PC, watching TV and doing paperwork in bed.

Are you wondering why? Well, according to the doctor, these activities will just stimulate the brain, instead of making you relaxed. Create the Right Environment- To create the right environment for sleep; you need to keep the room dark, at a moderate temperature and quiet.

Perform Some Mental Exercises – Having the ability to distract yourself from the things that keep you worried is enough to help you fall asleep more quickly. By simply performing a mental exercise, your brain will be able to concentrate away from all worries. Why don't you think of a beautiful beach resort with white sand, crystal clear blue waters and tall coconut trees, a wide green field, or a beautiful mansion with your favorite wall paint?

Concentrate on Positive Things – When you are in bed and notice that you keep on thinking negative thoughts, turn to more positive ones immediately. Obviously, negative thoughts will not do anything good to your entire well-being. Why don't you just focus on romantic or happy memories? Actually, this is the trick in having a good quality sleep.

Perform Relaxation Exercises – By regularly performing relaxation exercises, your racing thoughts and anxiety will be reduced. Two of the most common relaxation exercises that will give you refreshment are deep breathing and progressive muscle relaxation.
Take Part in Physical Activities – Performing regular physical exercise is also a great anxiety-reducer. However, ensure that you perform exercise a few hours before you go to bed, since it can be very stimulating.

What Boosts Your Anxiety or Steals Your Sleep? – If you find it hard falling asleep, you need to ask yourself on what habits interfere with your sleep of fuels your anxiety. In accordance with Dr. Epstein, the greatest sleep disruptors are alcohol and caffeine. The former acts as a sedative but it fragments the sleep cycle, making it less restful. On the other hand, the effects of the latter can last from 4-7 hours.

Consult a Sleep Specialist – If you feel like everything you have done is to no avail, you should start looking for a sleep specialist in your local area who performs cognitive-behavioral therapy. This is by far the most cost-effective treatment for any kinds of sleep disorder, as it only requires a few sessions and does not require any medication. There are specific sleep treatments, so it is crucial to see someone who is a certified and experienced sleep specialist.

These are just some of the best ways on how to shut off your brain before bedtime. If you are suffering from any sleep disorder like sleep apnea, insomnia or narcolepsy, why don't you try following them now?

Wrapping Up

When is it Time to Seek Professional Help?

If you can no longer bear the sleepless and restless nights brought by your sleep disorder and if you have already tried all the ways to get a good night's sleep but they did not seem to work, maybe it is about time to seek professional help. With the presence of sleep specialists and accredited sleep disorder centers, you can have a chance to get your sleep cycle back on track.

When to Seek Professional Help?

Before you finally decide to consult a sleep specialist or physician, you should first know when to do it. The following are some of the indicators:

- You can no longer remember the last time you had a good night's sleep
- You can count the hours you sleep on just one hand
- You find yourself waking up repeatedly through the night
- When you wake up, you feel like you are walking in a fog or going through the motions
- Your sleep deprivation affects your daily life at home, in school or at work
- You no longer enjoy the activities that you once loved to do
- You fall into deep sleep at inappropriate periods

What Does a Sleep Physician Do?

If you experience the abovementioned indicators, there is no doubt that you have to start looking for a qualified sleep specialist. But what does a sleep specialist do?

A sleep specialist has certification in the sleep medicine subspecialty and has specialization in the clinical evaluation, management, diagnosis, physiological testing and deterrence of circadian rhythm and sleep disorders.

A sleep specialist treats patients with the use of multidisciplinary approaches. The disorders that are managed by sleep specialists involve, but are not restricted to parasomnias, circadian rhythm disorders, sleep-related movement disorders, hypersomnia, insomnia and sleep-related breathing disorders.

If you feel like a living zombie due to sleepless and restless nights, don't prolong your agony anymore. By simply looking for a certified and experienced sleep specialist, you will be able to get the help you need. So, start looking for one now!